Buses, Coaches, Trolleybus & Recollections 195

Contents

Introduction   3

Leeds   4
Doncaster   13
Wath-upon-Dearne   15
Conisborough   16
Sheffield   17
Nottingham   21
Derby   24
Leicester   26
Wolverhampton   31
Coventry   34
London   36
Hastings   41
Brighton   44
Cardiff   48

1959 No 1 Records   16
1959 Happenings   32, 35, 44, 47
1959 Arrivals & Departures   47

Index of operators and vehicles   48

© Henry Conn 2015

First published in 2015
British Library Cataloguing in Publication Data

A catalogue record for this book is available from the British Library.

Acknowledgments

All the views in this book have come from the camera of John Clarke, and I am extremely grateful to John for access to this wonderful collection. My most sincere thanks to John – outstanding!

The PSV Circle fleet histories for the operators featured in this book, together with several issues of *Buses Illustrated*, were vital sources of information for the text.

ISBN 978 1 85794 458 7

Silver Link Publishing Ltd
The Trundle
Ringstead Road
Great Addington
Kettering
Northants NN14 4BW

Tel/Fax: 01536 330588
email: sales@nostalgiacollection.com
Website: www.nostalgiacollection.com

Printed and bound in the Czech Republic

Title page: **LEEDS** In 1950 90 Feltham cars were purchased by Leeds from the London Transport Executive. Car 2099 was the first to arrive, for trials in September 1949, entering passenger service in December. It retained its London fleet number until August 1950, when it became Leeds No 501. It is seen here at the Middleton auto sub-station on 28 March 1959. In December the tram passed to the British Transport Museum at Clapham, London, and is restored as Metropolitan Electric No 355.

About the author

My first recollections of public transport were early in 1958 in my home town of Aberdeen, travelling from our home in Mastrick to Union Street, then onwards by tram to Bridge of Dee. My interest in buses, trolleybuses and trams expanded to taking fleet numbers or registration numbers, and by the mid-1960s I had acquired a camera and began my collection. This interest continued through my family's moves from Aberdeen to Perth, Whitburn in West Lothian, Banbury, Swindon and Oxford by 1974.

My first job was with Customs & Excise, beginning in London with transfers to Oxford, Dover and Brighton. It was after I left Brighton that my enthusiasm for bus photography waned, and it never really returned apart from sporadic photography when I returned to Scotland in 1980. By this time I had left Customs & Excise and had returned to college in Cupar to study Agriculture. I met my future wife at this college and moved with her parents to Galloway, where I have lived very happily since 1983. To further my career I attended Aberdeen University to take a BSc Degree in Agriculture, and I successfully graduated in 1996. This led to me returning to the Civil Service with the Scottish Executive Rural Affairs Department, then through many changes to where I am now, working with Natural England as adviser to farmers on Environmental Schemes (three days a week from last July).

By 2010 I had a significant collection of transport views from the mid-1960s to the early 1980s. I met with Silver Link Publishing's editor Will Adams in Preston in early 2010 and was very kindly given the opportunity to write a volume on Buses, Trams and Trolleybuses in the Midlands. Since then I have continued to enjoy writing volumes on transport for Silver Link, this volume being my second in the 'Recollections' series looking at buses, trolleybuses and trams as well as significant events in a specific year.

Introduction

The year 1959 was one that changed everything, as it was the year when science and technology brought us the birth of the microchip, without which we would have no digital telephones, computers or satellites – there is almost nothing that we use in everyday life that does not use microchips.

1959 also brought the first step towards the birth control pill, which would help women to get jobs and advance professionally; research began in this year, but the pill was not available until the early 1960s.

It was the year Fidel Castro came to power in Cuba, the US Civil Rights Commission issued its withering report on racial discrimination in America, and the first American soldiers were killed in Vietnam.

Other 1959 events included the easing of relations between the USA and Russia, thanks to high-level diplomatic exchanges; scientists probing deeper into space; courts overturning literary censorship laws; and jazz musicians, painters and comedians debuting exciting new forms of expression. There was also a rising tide of politically tinged folk music.

Senator John F. Kennedy was laying the groundwork for what would turn out to be his successful run for the presidency the following year. Meanwhile Martin Luther King visited India and was deeply inspired by Gandhi. Six months after the death of architect Frank Lloyd Wright, the Guggenheim Museum, designed by him, opened its doors in New York. The Soviets and the USA both launched space probes to explore the remote corners of the solar system, and Motown Records released its first hit, *Money (That's What I Want)*.

At home, the end of January saw dense fog bringing chaos to Britain, and at the end of March 20,000 demonstrators attend a CND rally in Trafalgar Square. On 30 April an Icelandic gunboat fired on British trawlers in the first of the 'Cod Wars' over fishing rights. On 28 July postcodes were introduced to the UK for the first time, as an experiment, in the city of Norwich. In Lanarkshire, Scotland, 47 miners died as the result of an underground fire at Auchengeich Colliery on 18 September. Three weeks later 300 people needed to be rescued when a fire broke out on Southend Pier.

A General Election was held on 8 October 1959, and marked a third successive victory for the ruling Conservative Party, now led by Harold Macmillan. The Conservatives increased their overall majority again, to 100 seats over Hugh Gaitskell's Labour party.

On 2 November the first section of the M1 motorway was opened between Watford and Crick, near Rugby, and, significantly in the transport world, nine days later London Transport introduced the production AEC Routemaster into public service.

Enjoy the nostalgia!

LEEDS The 'Horsfield' cars entered service between 1930 and 1932 and were popular, with many new features such as flush side panels, 2 + 1 seating and air brakes. In Middleton Woods on 28 March 1959 is Horsfield car 179. To serve the growing population of the council estate, the Middleton Light Railway, an electric tramway, was built in 1925 by Leeds Corporation. From Leeds it ran parallel to the colliery line serving Hunslet Moor staithes, then headed south through Middleton Woods to a terminus on the Ring Road. The tramway was made into a circular route in 1949 when it was extended to Belle Isle Road and Balm Road in Hunslet.

Photo	**DESTINATIONS**
1	**LEEDS** (Title page)
2	**LEEDS** (Previous page)
3	**LEEDS**
4	**LEEDS**
5	**LEEDS**
6	**LEEDS**
7	**LEEDS**
8	**LEEDS**
9	**LEEDS**
10	**LEEDS**
11	**LEEDS**
12	**LEEDS**
13	**LEEDS**
14	**LEEDS**
15	**LEEDS**
16	**LEEDS**
17	**LEEDS**

LEEDS At Hunslet on 30 March 1959 is another Horsfield tram, No 181, which survived until the closure of the tramway system in Leeds.

A couple of months earlier film-maker Cecil B. DeMille died; he is remembered for many blockbuster movies such as The Ten Commandments, Samson and Delilah *and* The Greatest Show on Earth.

LEEDS Horsfield car 187 entered service in 1931, and is seen here in Belle Isle Road on 28 March 1959. No 187 would remain in the tramcar fleet until the end of operations on 7 November 1959, and was scrapped the following month.

Two days earlier performers at the Leeds Shaftesbury were Marty Wilde, Russ Conway, Cuddly Dudley, The Johnson Sisters and Colin and Christine Campbell; the compère was Bobby Dennis.

Left: **LEEDS** Working route 12 to Middleton on the same day as the previous picture is Horsfield No 189, a Brush car new in 1931. Numbers 180 and 189 exchanged numbers in April 1958; in January 1960 189 was acquired by the Tramway Museum Society at Crich and was later restored to its old number 180. Behind 180 is No 229 (5229 NW), a Roe-bodied Leyland PD3/5 new in early 1959.

On 26 March writer Raymond Chandler died. He is best known for the novels The Big Sleep, Farewell, My Lovely *and* The Long Goodbye, *featuring private eye Philip Marlowe.*

LEEDS On route 3 in Street Lane, also on 28 March 1959, is Horsfield car 197, which was scrapped three months later.

New television programmes in 1959 were Bonanza, The Twilight Zone *and* Rawhide *(who's not singing the* Rawhide *theme right now…?).*

Left: **LEEDS** In 1950 90 'Feltham' cars were purchased by Leeds from the London Transport Executive. The first of the UCC/1 type, which had been built for the Metropolitan Electric Tramways in 1930 and passed to the LTE on 1 July 1933, entered service in December 1949, retaining its London fleet number until August 1950, when it became Leeds No 501. Nos 502 to 550 entered service between October 1950 and August 1951. This view of 'Feltham' car 504 outside the Junction public house on Dewsbury Road and Moor Road was again taken on 28 March 1959.

Some Like It Hot, *the classic comedy starring Marilyn Monroe, Tony Curtis and Jack Lemmon, was released the next day.*

LEEDS At Crossgates, with the Regal cinema in the background, Feltham cars Nos 505 and 514 were photographed on the same day; 505 had been renumbered from 520 in August 1957. Both trams lasted until the end of tram operations and were broken up at Swinegate depot. The Regal Cinema was designed by A. V. Montague, built by Kenyon & Co and opened on 16 November 1936, providing seating for 1,500 and a car park for 400 vehicles, which at that time was the largest cinema car park in the UK. The first film was *Strike Me Pink* starring Eddie Cantor and Ethel Merman. The cinema closed on 11 January 1964, with John Wayne and Robert Mitchum starring in *The Longest Day*. The building was later demolished to make way for a supermarket.

It is possible that in 1959 the featured film at The Regal was The Thirty-Nine Steps *starring Kenneth More, a remake of the earlier Hitchcock version.*

LEEDS In Middleton Woods on the same day in 1959 is Feltham No 506 carrying a healthy number of passengers. This tram was still in stock on the last day of operation of the Leeds tramway system, and was scrapped by J. W. Hinchcliffe Ltd in Swinegate depot in January 1960.

3 February 1959 was dubbed 'The day the music died', when a plane crash killed musicians Buddy Holly, Ritchie Valens and the Big Bopper, as well as the pilot, near Clear Lake, Iowa. It Doesn't Matter Anymore by Buddy Holly was No 1 in the UK for three weeks from 9 April.

LEEDS In February 1959 Feltham car No 554, which had entered service with Leeds in November 1951, was renumbered 517. It is seen here at Leeds Bridge junction at 10.50 on the morning of 28 March.

TV's Juke Box Jury started on 1 June 1959, as well as Para Handy – Master Mariner, a series that followed the adventures of 'Clyde Puffer' The Vital Spark around the coastal waters of western Scotland, and the various schemes in which its wily skipper would get himself and his crew involved.

LEEDS Three hours later No 517 was photographed again, this time at Belle Isle. This car passed to the Middleton Railway Preservation Society in February 1960 but eventually became derelict following vandalism and was scrapped in April 1968. The bogies, however, were salvaged and are now in use on E1 tram No 1622 at Crich.

The Labour controlled Leeds Council finally decided to abandon the tramway system in Leeds, and on 28 March 1959 both the Middleton and Belle Isle routes were closed, an event known as 'The Dissolution of the Leeds Tram-car System'.

LEEDS The long reserved track sections on York Road and Selby Road, served by routes 18, 20 and 22, were frequent haunts of the Feltham trams. This is No 523 working route 18, also on 28 March; it remained in stock at the end of tram operations and was scrapped at Swinegate depot in February 1960.

Left: **LEEDS** Another view of No 523 on Moor Road on the same day.

The film Ben-Hur *was released on 18 November 1959. The famous chariot race sequence used an arena that took 1,000 workmen a year to carve out of a quarry at a cost of $1 million, and filming the race took five weeks spread over three months at a cost of a further $1 million.*

LEEDS Photographed at Halton also on 28 March 1959 is car 526. In early March 1960 this tram was exported to Seashore Railway, Kennebunkport, Maine, USA, where it remains. It had been offered to Seashore and had taken part in the last tram procession in November 1959. The former London Transport 2085, it is one of four British trams at Seashore, and is in a poor state. It is estimated that the cost of restoring it to passenger-carrying condition and repatriating it would be in excess of £700,000.

Left: **LEEDS** At Harehills Lane on the same day is Feltham car 549. It was withdrawn in July, sold to George Cohen and taken to a yard in Brown Lane, Holbeck, Leeds, to be scrapped. On arrival at the scrapyard, the car bodies were simply tipped off the trailers and set alight. The metal scrap was then recovered from the charred remains.

At this time, car ownership in the UK exceeded 30% of households.

LEEDS Working route 27 to Belle Isle on 27 March 1959 is Feltham car No 582, which had the distinction of being the last car to enter passenger service in Leeds on 31 July 1956. It was withdrawn in August 1959 and sold to George Cohen, to be scrapped at Brown Lane, Holbeck. The passing car is an Austin A35.

The A35 could achieve 60mph in 30 seconds and was flat out at 71mph. It ceased production in 1959 and was replaced by the A40 Farina models.

Left: **LEEDS** 7 November 1959 was a cold and foggy day in Leeds, and was the last day of tram operations in the city. At Crossgates on that day is a rather tired-looking No 501, which had been the first of the Felthams to be purchased in September 1949.

The No 1 UK single in November 1959 was Cliff Richard and the Shadows with Travellin' Light.

Photo	DESTINATIONS
18	DONCASTER
19	DONCASTER
20	DONCASTER
21	WATH-UPON-DEARNE
22	CONISBOROUGH
23	ROTHERHAM
24	SHEFFIELD
25	SHEFFIELD
26	SHEFFIELD
27	SHEFFIELD
28	SHEFFIELD
29	SHEFFIELD
30	SHEFFIELD
31	SHEFFIELD

DONCASTER trolleybus No 375 (CDT 636), a Karrier W that entered service in 1945 and was rebodied by Roe in 1955, is seen here on 1 April 1959. On 14 December 1963, as the only trolleybus remaining in service with the Corporation's Transport Department, it made the last trolleybus journeys to Beckett Road on the north-west side of Doncaster. On returning to the depot at the end of service, 35 years of trolleybus operation in the town finally came to an end.

On 2 April 1959 NASA announced the names of the seven men chosen as astronauts for Project Mercury, the first human spaceflight program of the United States, running from 1959 to 1963. The US reached its orbital goal on 20 February 1962, when John Glenn made three orbits around the Earth. When Project Mercury ended in May 1963, the US had sent six people into space.

DONCASTER At the end of the war Southend took delivery of nine Sunbeam Ws, Nos 130 to 138 (BHJ 827 to 829 and BHJ 898 to 903). No 130 was bodied by Brush and the remainder by Park Royal. At the end of 1953, Nos 130 to 138 were sold to Doncaster Corporation for £400 each, and all operated with their original bodies until rebodied by Roe between 1957 and 1959; between 1961 and 1962 these Roe bodies were transferred to Daimler CV bus chassis. In Wheatley Hills on 1 April 1959 is ex-Southend Sunbeam W No 392 (BHJ 903), showing off its new Roe body.

The average price of what we now call 4-star petrol from the Esso garage in the background in 1959 was 4s 9d a gallon (just under £5 at today's values). The average annual salary in 1959 was £496, or just over £10,000 today; in 2014 the average salary was about £26,000, so petrol was relatively expensive in 1959.

Below: **WATH-UPON-DEARNE** In 1948 Mexborough & Swinton took delivery of 12 Brush-bodied Sunbeam F4 trolleybuses, Nos 25 to 36 (FWX 909 to 920). Standing at Manvers terminus on 28 March 1959 is No 35 (FWX 919). The Mexborough system closed in 1961 and the 12 Sunbeam chassis, including that of No 35, minus their bodies, were acquired by Bradford. Five were used for spares and the other seven given new East Lancs bodies as fleet numbers 841 to 847. They were the last trolleybuses to be acquired by Bradford and the last to enter service in April 1961. No 35's chassis was one of those dismantled for spares in August 1961. Manvers Main Colliery in the background was closed on 25 March 1988 and the site later became home to one of the largest warehouses in Europe, belonging to Next.

At the time this view was taken Russ Conway was at No 1 with Side Saddle.

Above: **DONCASTER** London Transport RT155 HLW 142, a Park Royal-bodied AEC Regent III, entered service from Croydon depot in July 1947 working routes 115, 130 and 197. In September 1957 it entered Aldenham Works for overhaul and passed to North Street depot until withdrawn and stored in March 1958. In the same month the bus was acquired by Bird of Stratford-upon-Avon, then subsequently sold to Leon of Finningley in early 1959. HLW 142 remained in the Leon fleet until August 1966, and is seen here standing in Waterdale Bus Station, Doncaster, on 3 March 1959.

On this day Lou Costello of Abbott & Costello fame died, and a few months later his wife Anne died at the age of 47.

1959
No 1 Records

January
Jane Morgan — *The Day The Rains Came*
Elvis Presley — *One Night/I Got Stung*

February
Shirley Bassey — *As I Love You*

March
Platters — *Smoke Gets In Your Eyes*
Russ Conway — *Side Saddle*

April
Buddy Holly — *It Doesn't Matter Anymore*

May
Elvis Presley — *A Fool Such As I/I Need Your Love Tonight*

June
Russ Conway — *Roulette*

July
Bobby Darin — *Dream Lover*
Cliff Richard and the Drifters — *Living Doll*

September
Craig Douglas — *Only Sixteen*

October
Jerry Keller — *Here Comes Summer*
Bobby Darin — *Mack the Knife*
Cliff Richard and the Shadows — *Travellin' Light*

December
Adam Faith — *What Do You Want*
Emile Ford and the Checkmates — *What Do You Want To Make Those Eyes At Me For?*

CONISBOROUGH This is Mexborough & Swinton trolleybus No 30 (FWX 914), a Brush Sunbeam F4 new in 1948, at Conisborough High on 27 March 1959. Because of the predominance of low bridges in its operating area, the company's trolleybuses were all single-deck. In common with other post-war deliveries to the company, No 30 carried a 32-seat centre-entrance body by Brush. When acquired by Bradford in 1961, No 30 was one of those to be rebodied, becoming Bradford No 844. On 26 March 1972 No 844 fulfilled the role of Bradford's and Britain's last trolleybus when it was used to convey local dignitaries on the ceremonial last run. It was subsequently sold for preservation and moved to Sandtoft Transport Centre until May 1975, when it was purchased by the West Yorkshire Passenger Transport Executive, successors to Bradford City Transport. In 1984 it was placed on loan to the West Yorkshire Transport Museum, and on closure custodianship was transferred to Keighley Bus Museum Trust. No 844 still carries the commemorative lettering applied for that last run.

A few months after this view was taken, on 30 August, the Austin Mini went on sale for £500.

Right: **CONISBOROUGH** This is Rotherham Corporation trolleybus No 4 (FET 474), a Daimler CTE6 with East Lancs B38C bodywork new in 1949. Seen at Brook Square in Conisborough on 19 February 1959, No 4 is en route to Rotherham on the No 9 route operated jointly with Mexborough & Swinton.

On this day the UK decided to grant independence to Cyprus.

Below: **SHEFFIELD** All the following photographs of Sheffield trams were taken on 30 March 1959. Standing in the reserved track on Abbeydale Road South, the Beauchief terminus, is Standard car 191. The traffic lights on the right were activated by the trolley, causing the lights to turn red for other road users and giving priority to the tram to cross the road.

The 14th Dalai Lama, Tensin Gyatso, fled from Tibet on 17 March and was granted asylum in India on the 31st.

Below right: **SHEFFIELD** This is the triangular junction of Wicker and Blonk Street; the latter was a useful avoiding line for works access and football specials to Bramall Lane, and remained open until the end of the tramway system in Sheffield on 8 October 1960. On the right, heading for Millhouses, is Standard No 199, and travelling in the opposite direction to Weedon Street is domed-roof Standard 285.

Right: **SHEFFIELD** Passing Samuel Osborn & Co in Blonk Street is Standard car No 221. The bus in the background is an MCW-bodied AEC Regent V, new in 1956.

Below: **SHEFFIELD** At the Midland Station junction on Paternoster Row is Standard car No 87.

On 9 March 1959 the Barbie doll made her debut at the American International Toy Fair in New York.

Below right: **SHEFFIELD** This is the unmistakeable location of Sheffield Lane Top terminus, with Standard car No 208. The last tram from here, No 100, ran on 2 April 1960.

Below: **SHEFFIELD** Between 1950 and 1952 Nos 502 to 536 were constructed by Charles Roberts & Co of Horbury near Wakefield. They were carried on a four-wheel Maley & Taunton hornless type 588 truck with rubber and leaf spring suspension, powered by two Metrovick 101 DR3 65hp motors. Air brakes were fitted, acting on all wheels, and electric braking was available for emergency use. On Firth Park Road is Roberts car No 535. In the background is Firth Park Lodge and Pavilion, which dates from the mid-19th century and is now a Grade II listed building.

Above: **SHEFFIELD** Framed by the Wicker arches is domed-roof Standard car No 261. The famous bridge was built in 1848 by Sir John Fowler and survives as today as a Grade II listed structure.

Sheffield's Norfolk Market Hall was closed on 30 June 1959, when part of the Castle Market was opened in order to accommodate the traders.

SHEFFIELD The prototype for the Roberts cars, No 501, was built at Queens Road Works in August 1946.
With comfortable upholstered seating for 62 passengers, it was the last car to be built at the works.

Photo	DESTINATIONS
32	NOTTINGHAM
33	NOTTINGHAM
34	NOTTINGHAM
35	NOTTINGHAM
36	NOTTINGHAM
37	NOTTINGHAM
38	NOTTINGHAM
39	NOTTINGHAM
40	DERBY
41	DERBY
42	LEICESTER
43	LEICESTER
44	LEICESTER
45	LEICESTER
46	WOLVERHAMPTON
47	WOLVERHAMPTON
48	WOLVERHAMPTON
49	WOLVERHAMPTON
50	COVENTRY
51	COVENTRY

Above: **NOTTINGHAM** At Trent Bridge on 12 September 1959 are Nos 551 (KTV 551) on the right and 533 (KTV 533), both Brush-bodied BUT 9641Ts. No 533 was new in November 1950 and 551 in January 1951, and both were withdrawn in 1965.

According to the Nottinghamshire County Cricket report, the season of 1959 will long be remembered for its fine weather. Trent Bridge hosted the first test with India between 4 and 8 June, and the third test against South Africa between 7 and 12 July.

Right: **NOTTINGHAM** At Victoria Embankment on the same day is No 580 (KTV 580), another of the Brush-bodied BUT 9641Ts new in December 1951.

Two days later Luna 2 became the first man-made object to crash on the Moon, and on the same day Morten Harket of Norwegian group A-Ha was born.

NOTTINGHAM Standing at Cinderhill on 29 August 1959 is No 585 (KTV 585), which was new in February 1952 and sold for scrap in December 1965. These Brush-bodied BUT 9641Ts were 7ft 6in wide and fitted with an English Electric EE410/4B 120hp motor.

On this day the Casbah Coffee Club, located at West Derby in suburban Liverpool, opened for business. The Les Stewart Quartet had been scheduled to play on the opening night, but the group broke up after an argument. Instead, Quartet members George Harrison and Ken Brown teamed up with two members of the Quarrymen, John Lennon and Paul McCartney, and the four guitarists played the opener. Dissatisfied with the pay, Brown quit the Quarrymen after six weeks, while Lennon, McCartney and Harrison went on to greater fame.

NOTTINGHAM At Wollaton Park at 1.30 on the afternoon of the same day is similar tram No 582 (KTV 582), new in December 1951 and scrapped in February 1966.

On this day actress Rebecca de Mornay was born in Santa Rosa, California.

NOTTINGHAM In King Edward Street, also on 29 August, is No 489 (KTV 489), a Roe-bodied BUT 9611T new in November 1948. It was battery-manoeuvrable and was initially to have had MCCW bodywork, but it was changed to Roe due to delays in delivery. No 489 was sold for scrap in May 1965.

The first fatal crash of a passenger jet killed five American Airlines crewmen, who were on a training flight in a Boeing 707. The crew were practising landings at a private airfield owned by Grumman Aircraft when the jet crashed in a potato field.

Left: **NOTTINGHAM** This is Wilford Road on 12 September 1959, and working route 47 is No 475 (HAU 175), a Park Royal-bodied Karrier W new in March 1946. It was scrapped in Larkhall, Scotland, in May 1963.

Bonanza appeared for the first time on American television, premiering at 7.30pm Eastern time on NBC. The western, the first to be broadcast in colour, ran for 14 seasons and 440 episodes until 16 January 1973.

Below: **NOTTINGHAM** The Central Market in the background opened in 1928, and closed in 1972 when the Victoria Centre Market opened. On route 40 on 12 September 1959 is No 460 (GTV 660), a Roe-bodied Karrier W new in March 1945; it would be sold for scrap after 20 years' service in June 1965. The car ahead of it is an Austin A30, which had a smaller rear window than the A35.

On 8 September Prime Minister Harold Macmillan announced that new elections for the 630 seats in the House of Commons would take place on 8 October, with Parliament to be dissolved on 18 September.

Above: **NOTTINGHAM** Also working the same route on that day is sister trolleybus No 469 (HAU 169). New in March 1946, all ten in the batch had utility bodies with upholstered seats. No 469 was sold for scrap in July 1965.

The first successful plain paper copying machine, the Xerox 914, was introduced at a show at the Sherry-Netherland Hotel in New York four days after this photograph was taken.

DERBY Between December 1948 and January 1949 Derby took delivery of 11 Brush-bodied Sunbeam F4s, Nos 186 to 196 (ARC 486 to 496). At Balaclava Road on 5 September 1959 is No 190 (ARC 490), which was withdrawn and sold for scrap in December 1966.

Appearing at the Derby Gaumont on 27 September that year were Johnny Wiltshire and the Trebletones, and Cliff Richard and the Shadows.

DERBY Travelling along Nottingham Road on the same day is Willowbrook-bodied Sunbeam F4 No 224 (DRC 224), one of a batch of nine that were new between November 1952 and January 1953. No 224 was the last official Derby trolleybus on 9 September 1967, and was purchased for preservation that month; it is now in the East Anglia Transport Museum.

Right: **LEICESTER** Bus Station was visited on 15 August 1959, when these pictures were taken. In September 1947 RT420 (HLX 237), a Weymann roof-box AEC Regent III, began work in London and was allocated to Old Kent Road depot for most of its service life. During June 1958 it was sold to Bird of Stratford-upon-Avon, and in the same month it was purchased by Brown's Blue Coaches of Markfield, which fitted it with platform doors. The bus is seen at St Margaret's Bus Station, Leicester. In March 1963 it was purchased by Super Coaches of Upminster, but was damaged in an accident in December of that year and later sold for scrap. In the background is RT157 (HLW 144), also acquired through Bird's at the same time; this bus went on to be purchased by Simpson's of Rosehearty in March 1963, then acquired by Alexander Northern with the business in November 1966, and was withdrawn in December 1968.

On this day Cyprus gained independence.

Left: **LEICESTER** In 1950 Kemp & Shaw Ltd of Leicester took delivery of GRY 763, an all-Leyland PD2/1. The business was taken over by Midland Red in August 1955, but its buses retained the Kemp & Shaw livery until December 1958, when the company was liquidated. Seen here in the bus station, it is in Midland Red livery and carries the fleet number 4844, and can be compared with the Midland Red Brush-bodied AD2 No 3117 (JHA 18) beside it, new in 1946.

Eleven days after this view was taken the Mini, designed by Sir Alec Issigonis, was launched.

LEICESTER exchanged six Weymann-bodied AEC Regal buses from Devon General with six AEC Regent IIs in July 1952, and the acquired Regals were allocated fleet numbers 195 to 200 (HTT 484/486/487/498/502/504). Leaving St Margaret's Bus Station on the Inner Circle, on which all the Regals worked, is No 195 (HTT 484). It was withdrawn in December 1963 and acquired by Tiger Coaches of Salsburgh.

LEICESTER At The Newarke, we see No 2140 (EHA 272), one of Midland Red's unique pre-war front-entrance FEDD double-deckers. They were built in large numbers between 1933 and 1939 with bodywork by Carlyle, Short Brothers, Metro-Cammell and Brush, then were extensively rebuilt by Hooton Aero Engineering in the 1940s to extend their working lives. The last FEDDs were withdrawn in December 1960.

The day before this view was taken, basketball player Magic Johnson was born in Michigan.

WOLVERHAMPTON

These Wolverhampton trolleybuses were photographed on 26 September 1959. At its peak in 1959-60, the city's trolleybus system had several routes covering the borough and beyond. At Bushbury Hill is No 468 (FJW 468), a Park Royal-bodied Sunbeam F4 new in 1948.

Two weeks before this view was taken Marty Wilde appeared at the Gaumont in Wolverhampton.

1959 Happenings (1)

WOLVERHAMPTON trolleybus routes 12 and 13 ran from Finchfield/Merry Hill to Wolverhampton and Low Hill. At Merry Hill is No 413 (DJW 943), a Park Royal-bodied Sunbeam W4 new in 1945.

Typhoon Vera hit central Honshu, Japan, killing more than 5,000, injuring another 39,000, and leaving 1,500,000 homeless. Also on this day the first large unit action of the Vietnam War took place.

January
Tyne Tees Television goes on air in the North East of England
The USSR successfully launches Luna 1 moon probe
Rebel troops led by Che Guevara enter city of Havana, followed shortly by Fidel Castro
Charles De Gaulle inaugurated as first president of French Fifth republic
Motown Records founded by Berry Gordy Jnr

February
UK grants Cyprus its independence
Prime Minister Harold Macmillan holds talks with Soviet leader Nikita Khrushchev in USSR
First successful test firing of Titan intercontinental ballistic missile from Cape Canaveral, Florida
Fidel Castro becomes Premier of Cuba

March
Large CND demonstration in Trafalgar Square
Archbishop Makarios returns to Cyprus from exile
Dalai Lama flees Tibet and is granted asylum in India
Debut of the Barbie doll

April
Official name of administrative county Hampshire changed from 'County of Southampton' to 'County of Hampshire'
United Dairies merges with Cow & Gate to form Unigate Dairies
Icelandic gunboat fires on British trawlers in first of 'Cod Wars'
St Lawrence Seaway opens, linking Great Lakes with Atlantic Ocean

Left: **WOLVERHAMPTON** Route 59 ran from Wolverhampton through Wood End to Wednesfield, and working this route in Broad Street is No 418 (DUK 18), a Sunbeam W4 with Park Royal bodywork new in 1945.

Below: **WOLVERHAMPTON** Working route 58 between Wolverhampton and Dudley is No 623 (FJW 623), a Park Royal-bodied Sunbeam F4 new in 1950. The car in full view is a Singer Gazelle, which in 1959 cost £956 including taxes.

The No 1 UK single in September 1959 was Only Sixteen by Craig Douglas, and the No 1 album for the whole of 1959 was the soundtrack to South Pacific.

May
First Ten Tors event held on Dartmoor
FA Cup Final at Wembley: Nottingham Forest beat Luton Town 2-1
Mermaid Theatre opens in City of London
Gypsy, musical starring Ethel Merman, opens on Broadway and runs for 702 performances
Monkeys 'Able' and 'Miss Baker' became first living beings to successfully return to Earth from space aboard Jupiter spacecraft

June
First showing of BBC TV's *Juke Box Jury*, chaired by David Jacobs
Singapore granted self-governing status
Hovercraft, invented by Christopher Cockerell, officially launched
USS *George Washington*, first submarine to carry ballistic missiles, launched

COVENTRY During 1951 Coventry Corporation took delivery of No 100 (GKV 100), an MCCW-bodied Crossley DD42/7T. It originally had a turbo-transmitter, and was fitted with a 7.7-litre AEC engine and crash gearbox in October 1953; it was further converted in December 1961, receiving the engine, gearbox and transmission from Daimler CWA6 No 352 (EKV 952). No 100 is seen here in Broadgate on 22 August 1959 painted in its reverse livery, which it retained throughout its existence, being withdrawn and sold for scrap in May 1965.

1959 Happenings (2)

COVENTRY Working service 5 to Coundon in Corporation Street on the same day is No 18 (FHP 18), an MCCW-bodied Daimler CVA6 new in 1948. No 18 was withdrawn in 1965 and became a driver trainer until December 1967, when it was sold for scrap.

On 18 May 1959, appearing for a week at the Coventry Theatre were Lonnie Donegan and his Skiffle Group and Des O'Connor, billed as 'new-style comedy'. On 16 September 1959 Cliff Richard and the Shadows were appearing at the city's Gaumont Theatre.

July

UK postcodes first introduced, experimentally in Norwich

Mental Health Act, modernising care of mental disorders, and Obscene Publications Act become law

At opening of American National Exhibition in Moscow, US Vice President Richard Nixon and USSR Premier Nikita Khrushchev engage in 'Kitchen Debate'

August

Barclays becomes first bank to install a computer

House of Fraser acquires Harrods for £37 million

First Mini goes on sale

PM Harold Macmillan and US President Eisenhower make joint TV broadcast from Downing Street

US spacecraft Explorer 6 sends first picture of Earth from orbit

Hawaii is admitted as 50th US state

September

USSR's Luna 2 becomes first man-made object to crash on Moon

USSR Premier Nikita Khrushchev and his wife tour US at invitation of President Eisenhower

Xerox 914, first plain paper copier, introduced to public

First official large unit action of Vietnam War takes place, when US troops are ambushed by Vietcong force

Photo	DESTINATIONS
52	LONDON
53	LONDON
54	LONDON
55	LONDON
60	LONDON
61	LONDON
62	LONDON
63	LONDON
64	LONDON
65	LONDON
66	LONDON
67	LONDON
68	LONDON
69	LONDON
70	LONDON

LONDON This is the Frays Bridge, the Uxbridge terminus of route 607, and leaving the terminus for Shepherds Bush on 21 July 1959 is F1 No 715 (DLY 715); in the background is AEC trolleybus tower TXV 907. Uxbridge was the westernmost place reached by the London trolleybus system and was operated by Hanwell depot until the last day of operations on 8 November 1960.

LONDON Route 667 ran between Hammersmith and Hampton Court, and travelling along Stanley Road, Fulwell, on 30 December 1959 is Q1 No 1778 (HYM 778).

On this day Tracy Ullman was born in Slough, and the Christmas No 1 in the UK was Emile Ford and the Checkmates with What Do You Want To Make Those Eyes At Me For?.

Above: **LONDON** Route 662 worked from Sudbury to Paddington, and at Sudbury & Harrow Road station on Harrow Road on 3 April 1959 is C3 No 298 (CUL 298). The car passing the trolleybus is a Nash Metropolitan, which was produced between 1953 and 1961 and assembled in Longbridge, Birmingham.

Three weeks after this view was taken the St Lawrence Seaway linking the Great Lakes and the Atlantic Ocean officially opened to shipping.

Right: **LONDON** With the now listed St Pancras station hotel building in the background, and working route 513 to Parliament Fields on 2 July 1959, is No 1045 (EXV 45).

Two days after this view was taken, following the admission of Alaska as the 49th state earlier in the year, the 49-star flag of the United States made it debut in Philadelphia.

Above: **LONDON** Working the 643 route to Wood Green at High Holborn on 25 March 1959 is K2 trolleybus No 1229 (EXV 229). The AEC Regent working to Marylebone is RT 1706 (KYY 533), which entered service from Holloway depot in April 1950 and at the time of this view was working out of Barking depot; 1706 would be sold for scrap in December 1978.

Right: **LONDON** Captured in a Field Marshal's uniform and holding aloft a cocked hat, the statue of Prince Albert in Holborn Circus was presented to the City of London by merchant Charles Oppenheim. Designed by Charles Bacon the statue was unveiled in 1874, 13 years after Albert's death. Passing the statue on route 617 to North Finchley on 23 June 1959 is No 1554 (FXH 554).

On this day, convicted Manhattan Project spy Klaus Fuchs was released after only nine years in a British prison and allowed to emigrate to Dresden, East Germany, where he resumed a scientific career.

Below: **LONDON** At the Angel, Islington, on 14 April 1959 is K2 trolleybus No 1312 (EXV 312), heading for the Ming Street terminus of route 677 at West India Docks.

Below: **LONDON** Working route 643 to Holborn Circus at Bruce Grove, Tottenham, on 26 November 1959 is No 1224 (EXV 224).

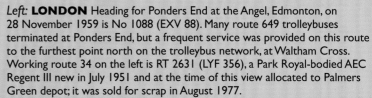

Left: **LONDON** Heading for Ponders End at the Angel, Edmonton, on 28 November 1959 is No 1088 (EXV 88). Many route 649 trolleybuses terminated at Ponders End, but a frequent service was provided on this route to the furthest point north on the trolleybus network, at Waltham Cross. Working route 34 on the left is RT 2631 (LYF 356), a Park Royal-bodied AEC Regent III new in July 1951 and at the time of this view allocated to Palmers Green depot; it was sold for scrap in August 1977.

Below left: **LONDON** This is Ponders End on that same November day, and about to work route 649 to Liverpool Street is No 1157 (EXV 157). To the right is AEC Routemaster RM 56 (VLT 56), which had entered service from Tottenham on routes 34B and 76 in September, and would be transferred to Upton Park at the end of November for training purposes, spending most of its service life at West Ham depot.

Below: **LONDON** Woodford was the northern terminus of route 581, and Lea Bridge depot had the majority of vehicles allocated to this route. Turning from Mare Street at Hackney station and heading for Bloomsbury, the southern terminus of the route, on 13 April 1959 is K2 No 1343 (EXV 343).

Right: **LONDON** Route 557 operated between Liverpool Street station and Chingford Mount, and emerging from Hackney Road at Cambridge Heath station on 8 April 1959 is K1 No 1065 (EXV 65). Turning right into Cambridge Heath Road is a Bedford CA Dormobile. The first CAs featured a two-piece windscreen comprising two separate flat sheets of glass separated by a central vertical metal divide. As curved screen glass became available in the UK at an acceptable price, the two-piece windscreen was replaced with a single slightly curved windscreen in approximately 1958.

Below: **LONDON** Walthamstow and West Ham depots jointly operated route 697 between Chingford Mount and the Victoria & Albert Docks. At Stratford Broadway, with Stratford Town Hall in the background, heading for Chingford Mount on 9 July 1959 is No 1658 (FXH 658).

On this day, Jim Kerr of Simple Minds was born in Glasgow.

Right: **LONDON** Route 647 operated between Stamford and London Docks, and on 13 April 1959 in Leman Street, Whitechapel (famous as the location of the police station in TV's *Ripper Street*) we see K1 No 1109 (EXV 109).

On this day the Vatican forbade Roman Catholics from voting for communists, the US Air Force launched Discoverer II *into polar orbit, and the film* Warlock *with Richard Widmark and Henry Fonda was released.*

Below: **LONDON** On route 665 to Bloomsbury in London Road, Barking, on 23 May 1959 is L3 No 1448 (FXH 448).

Bob Mortimer, best known for his double act with Vic Reeves, was born on this day. Before 1959, 24 May was known as British Empire Day, but was renamed Commonwealth Day in that year.

Photo	DESTINATIONS
71	HASTINGS
72	HASTINGS
73	HASTINGS
74	HASTINGS
75	HASTINGS
76	HASTINGS
77	BRIGHTON
78	BRIGHTON
79	BRIGHTON
80	BRIGHTON
81	BRIGHTON
82	BRIGHTON
83	BRIGHTON
84	BRIGHTON
85	CARDIFF

Above right: **HASTINGS** was visited on 16 May 1959, to photograph some of the town's trolleybuses. On 1 October 1957 Maidstone & District acquired the Hastings Tramway Company, but the trolleybuses retained their Hastings fleet numbers. This is Maidstone & District No 13 (BDY 788), a Park Royal-bodied AEC 661T new in June 1940, on Ivyhouse Lane. The trolleybus was scrapped by Winchester & Sons at Silverhill depot less than three months after this picture was taken. The car is a Sunbeam Talbot 90 Mark II dating from 1950 to 1952.

Elvis Presley had the No 1 single in May 1959 with A Fool Such as I.

Above: **HASTINGS** Working the Circular Route 2 is No 22 (BDY 797), a Park Royal-bodied Sunbeam W4 new in January 1946. This trolleybus was purchased by Bradford Corporation in July 1959, and eventually sold for scrap in April 1964. To the right is identical No 24 on route 6; this vehicle was also purchased by Bradford in July 1959 and also sold for scrap in April 1964.

Above: **HASTINGS** Working route 8 to Bexhill at Alexandra Park, Hastings, is No 43 (BDY 818), a Weymann bodied Sunbeam W4 new in June 1948; 43 would pass to Maidstone Corporation in May 1959 and was sold for scrap in April 1967.

Right: **HASTINGS** Passing the Royal Sussex Arms on Old London Road is No 5 (BDY 780), a Weymann-bodied AEC 661T new in June 1940.

On 18 May 1959, hours after his divorce from Elaine Davis became final, Mickey Rooney married his fifth wife, Barbara Ann Thomson. The New York Daily News *headline read 'Half-Pint Takes a Fifth'.*

On 30 May the first trial of a British hovercraft took place at Cowes on the Isle of Wight.

Above: **HASTINGS** This is Maidstone & District No 2 (BDY 777), a Weymann-bodied AEC 661T new in June 1940, working route 6 to Ore. No 2 would be scrapped at Silverhill depot just a few weeks after this view was taken.

On 12 May 1959, hours after his divorce from Debbie Reynolds became final, Eddie Fisher married Elizabeth Taylor in Las Vegas.

Right: **HASTINGS** Heading for Silverhill on route 6 is No 19 (BDY 794), a Park Royal-bodied AEC 661T new in June 1940, which was scrapped at Silverhill in July 1959. In the background can be seen one of the Weymann-bodied Leyland PDR1/1s that replaced the trolleybuses.

BRIGHTON The first trolleybuses in Brighton were placed in service on 1 May 1939 on route 48, and the first trolleybus in service was No 3. However, the opening ceremony was not held until 1 June, with No 1 decorated with flags and having its tyres painted white for the occasion. Brighton Corporation No 1 (FUF 1), a Weymann-bodied AEC 661T new in March 1939, is seen here at the Royal Pavilion on 30 July 1959; it was in service on the last day of trolleybuses on 30 June 1961 and was scrapped a month later.

1959 Happenings (3)

October
- 300 people rescued from fire on Southend Pier
- UK General Election results in record third successive Conservative victory, with increased majority of 100 seats; one of new MPs is Margaret Thatcher
- Ronnie Scott's Jazz Club opens in Soho
- US TV anthology series *The Twilight Zone* premieres on CBS
- USSR probe Luna 3 sends back first ever photos of far side of the Moon
- First appearance of cartoon character Astérix the Gaul

The No 1 single in the UK was Cliff Richard and the Drifters with Living Doll (written by Lionel Bart). At the end of 1959 the Drifters became the Shadows, to avoid confusion with the US group of the same name.

Below: **BRIGHTON** At Race Hill on route 43A, with blinds set for the return journey to Old Steine on 24 March 1959, is Brighton Corporation No 6 (FUF 6), a Weymann bodied AEC 661T new in 1939 and still available for service at the end of trolleybus operations in the town. Wrigley's was founded on 1 April 1891, originally selling products such as soap and baking powder. In 1892 the company began packaging chewing gum with each can of baking powder; the gum eventually became more popular than the baking powder and Wrigley's reoriented the company towards the new product.

Six days after this photograph was taken, 20,000 demonstrators attend a Campaign for Nuclear Disarmament rally in Trafalgar Square.

Right: **BRIGHTON** Travelling along the tree-lined Surrenden Road on 30 July 1959 is No 15 (FUF 15), another of the Weymann-bodied AEC 661Ts new in 1939. This was one of six Brighton trolleybuses (Nos 10 to 15) loaned to Newcastle-upon-Tyne Corporation between 1942 and 1946, being used on route 9.

Below: **BRIGHTON** En route to the Aquarium at Beaconsfield Villas on Preston Drove on the same day is sister trolleybus No 31 (FUF 31). The estate car in the background is a Standard Vanguard.

Five days earlier the SRN1 hovercraft had crossed the English Channel from Dover to Calais in just over 2 hours.

Below right: **BRIGHTON** No 44 (FUF 44) was numerically the last of the batch of 44 Weymann-bodied AEC 661Ts delivered to Brighton between March and September 1939, and is seen here in Surrenden Road, also on 30 July 1959.

The Lenin was the first nuclear-powered surface ship, and entered operation in 1959 working to clear sea routes of ice for cargo ships along Russia's northern coast. From 1960 to 1965 she covered more than 85,000 miles during the Arctic navigation season, of which almost 65,000 were through ice.

Left: **BRIGHTON** The 41 and 42 were circular routes that turned right at the Junction, Queens Park Road, to Rock Gardens, Old Steine. The 41 route then went straight up Lewes Road to Elm Grove, whereas the 42 went via North Road and Queens Road to the station, round to Seven Dials, then via Preston Circus and the Open Market. Working the 41 at Queens Park on 24 March 1959 is CPM 61, a Weymann-bodied AEC 661T that entered service in January 1945.

The Platters' Smoke Gets In Your Eyes *had been the No 1 single the week before this view was taken.*

Below left: **BRIGHTON** Under a pooling agreement with Brighton Corporation dated 1 April 1939, Brighton Hove & District had power to operate up to 20% of the total trolleybus mileage. In 1939 eight trolleybuses were purchased by BH&D, but the war intervened and they were stored until 1945/46. One of the batch was CPM 521, a Weymann-bodied AEC 661T that had entered service in December 1945. Also in view at Brighton station on 24 March 1959 is BH&D's GNJ 996, an ECW-bodied Bristol K6B new in 1948.

Cliff Richard and the Drifters appeared at Brighton Dome on 16 January 1959.

Below: **BRIGHTON** 24 March 1959 was the last day of trolleybus services on the 41, 42 and 48 routes, and working a 48 service on that day is No 24 (FUF 24), a Weymann-bodied AEC 661T new in 1939. It was sold for scrap in May.

On 18 March President Dwight D. Eisenhower signed the bill allowing Hawaii to become the 50th state of the United States of America.

1959 Happenings (4)

November

First section of M1 motorway, and M45 and M10 spurs, opened between Watford and Crick, near Rugby, following ceremony near Toddington by Minister of Transport Ernest Marples

London Transport introduces production Routemaster buses into public service

Prestwick and Renfrew become first UK airports with duty-free shops

Britain becomes founder member of European Free Trade Association

MGM epic *Ben-Hur* is released and becomes studio's greatest hit so far, later winning a record 11 Academy Awards

December

First episode of children's animated TV programme *Ivor the Engine*, made by Oliver Postgate and Peter Firmin's Smallfilms

In first Cold War arms control treaty, 12 countries, including USA and USSR, agree to set aside Antarctica as scientific preserve and ban military activity there

Makarios III selected as first President of independent Cyprus

1959 Arrivals & Departures

Arrivals

Sade (Helen Folasade Adu)	Singer	16 January
Linda Blair	Actress	22 January
Vic Reeves	Comedian and actor	24 January
Lol Tolhurst	Musician (The Cure)	3 February
Renée Fleming	American soprano	14 February
John McEnroe	Tennis player	16 February
Nick Griffin	Politician, BNP	1 March
Steve McFadden	*EastEnders* actor	20 March
David Hyde Pierce	Actor (*Frasier*)	3 April
Emma Thompson	Actress and screenwriter	15 April
Sean Bean	Actor	17 April
Robert Smith	Musician (The Cure)	21 April
Paula Yates	TV presenter	24 April
Sheena Easton	Singer	27 April
Ben Elton	Comedian and writer	3 May
Ian McCulloch	Musician	5 May
Paul Whitehouse	Comedian	17 May
(Stephen) Morrissey	Musician	22 May
Bob Mortimer	Comedian	23 May
Rupert Everett	Actor	29 May
Martin Brundle	Motor racing driver/commentator	1 June
Hugh Laurie	Actor and musician	11 June
Sophie Grigson	Cookery writer and chef	19 June
Julie Birchill	Journalist	3 July
Jim Kerr	Musician (Simple Minds)	9 July
Kevin Spacey	Actor and director	26 July
Jeanette Winterson	Novelist	27 August
Morten Harket	Singer (A-Ha)	14 September
Greg Proops	Comedian	3 October
Simon Cowell	Music producer	7 October
Kirsty MacColl	Singer/songwriter	10 October
Marie Osmond	Singer	13 October
Sarah Ferguson	Duchess of York	15 October
Gary Kemp	Musician and actor	16 October
Niamh Cusack	Actress	20 October
Peter Mullan	Actor	2 November
Bryan Adams	Singer	5 November
Paul McGann	Actor	14 November
Charles Kennedy	Politician	25 November
Lorraine Kelly	Presenter and journalist	30 November
Gwyneth Strong	Actress	2 December
Jasper Conran	Fashion designer	12 December
Andy McNab	Soldier and novelist	28 December
Tracey Ullman	Comedian, actress and writer	30 December
Val Kilmer	Actor	31 December

Departures

Cecil B. DeMille	Film director (b1881)	21 January
Mike Hawthorn	Racing driver (b1929)	22 January
The Big Bopper (J. P. Richardson)	Musician (b1930)	3 February
Buddy Holly	Musician (b1936)	3 February
Ritchie Valens	Musician (b1941)	3 February
Lou Costello	Actor and comedian (b1906)	3 March
Raymond Chandler	Novelist (b1888)	26 March
Frank Lloyd Wright	Architect (b1867)	9 April
John Foster Dulles	US politician (b1888)	24 May
Charles Vidor	Film director (b1900)	4 June
Ethel Barrymore	Actress (b1879)	18 June
Billie Holiday	Singer (b1915)	17 July
Jacob Epstein	Sculptor (b1880)	19 August
Bohuslav Martinu	Czech composer (b1890)	28 August
Gerard Hoffnung	Humorist (b1925)	25 September
Errol Flynn	Actor (b1909)	14 October
Heitor Villa-Lobos	Brazilian composer (b1887)	17 November
Stanley Spencer	Painter (b1891)	14 December

CARDIFF Clarence Bridge, which crosses the River Taff in Cardiff, was named after the Duke of Clarence and completed in 1890. Crossing it on 31 December 1959 is Cardiff No 247 (EBO 904), an East Lancashire-bodied BUT 9641T new in 1950. It was withdrawn in 1966 and sold for scrap.

Index of operators and vehicles

Brighton, Hove & District: GNJ 996 46
Brighton: FUF 1, FUF 6 44; FUF 15, FUF 31, FUF 44 45; CPM 61, FUF 24 46
Brown's Blue Coaches: HLX 237 28

Cardiff: EBO 904 48
Coventry: GKV 100 34; FHP 18 35

Derby: ARC 490 26; DRC 224 27
Doncaster: CDT 636 13; BHJ 903 14

Kemp & Shaw (Midland Red): GRY 763

Leeds tramcars: 179 3; 181 4; 187, 189 5; 197 6; 501 1, 12; 504 6; 505, 506 7; 517 8, 9; 523 10; 526, 549 11; 582 12
Leicester: HTT 484 29
Leon of Finningley: HLW 142 15
London: DLY 715, HYM 778 36; CUL 298, EXV 45, EXV 229 37; EXV 312, EXV 224, FXH 554 38;

EXV 88, EXV 157, EXV 343 39; EXV 65, EXV 109, FXH 658 40; FXH 448 41

Maidstone & District (Hastings): BDY 788 41; BDY 780, BDY 797, BDY 818 42; BDY 777, BDY 794 43
Mexborough & Swinton: FWX 919 15; FWX 914 16
Midland Red: JHA 18 28; EHA 272 30

Nottingham: KTV 533, KTV 551, KTV 580 21; KTV 585 22; KTV 582 23; KTV 489, HAU 175 24; HAU 169, GTV 660 25

Rotherham: FET 474 17

Sheffield tramcars: 191, 199, 285 17; 87, 208, 221 18; 261, 535 19; 501 20

Wolverhampton: FJW 468 31; DJW 943 32; DUK 18, FJW 623 33

Front cover: **BRIGHTON** At Upper Rock Gardens on the last day of trolleybus operations of the 41 Circular on 24 March 1959 is Brighton Hove & District No 346 (CPM 521), an AEC 661T with Weymann bodywork, which entered service in December 1945. Films on release in March 1959 included *Room at the Top, Some Like It Hot, Al Capone,* and the John Wayne western *Rio Bravo.*